Land Sea Earth Sky

Scripture in Haiku

TRACY ANN JOHNSON, Ed.D

xulon
PRESS

www.xulonpress.com

TABLE OF CONTENTS

ACKNOWLEDGEMENT

I would like to first thank my mighty and wonderful Father in heaven, the Lord Jesus Christ, the King of all Kings. "He Doeth all things well" and he has been so gracious and kind, delivering me out of impossible places, spiritually, mentally and physically. He gave me a love for writing, especially poetry, and I thank Him for that.

Secondly, I thank my husband, children, grand-children, siblings and their spouses whom God has planted in my life. They have been and continue to be supportive of my creative endeavors, showing me love through my mistakes and sometimes quirky personality. They have always cheered me on.

Thirdly, I thank my friends who have been just like my family, encouraging me to grow in my writing life and in other areas of my Christian walk. I thank God for placing them in my path.

This book is dedicated to all of them, with special thanks to those who gave helpful feedback.

INTRODUCTION

*I*n the middle of the night, the Voice whis-
pered to me, "Land Sea Earth Sky." I had
been contemplating doing a book of Christian
poetry for some time, but kept procrastinating,
perhaps out of fear of failure or maybe because
periodically I am honestly lazy. But mostly, in this
case, it was fear. To make myself begin this project,
which for me became a labor of love, I listened
to the Voice, got out of bed and went to my com-
puter. I knew this was a title for something. I knew
also I had a stack of poems, all different genres,
lying dormant in various boxes, file cabinets, loose

folders, surprisingly organized binders and on top of my printer in my small office.

I began to riffle through my cache of poetry, old and new, and kept picking up the haikus, specifically the collection I named "My Kind of Haiku". I love this Japanese form of poetry. I love writing it, reading it and teaching it to students from middle school to college level. I found that haiku was a great fear-proof introduction to poetry, which most middle school boys loathed unless it was Rap and most adults on the college level detested because they did not think they could write it. To many of them, poetry was a rhyme-only exercise. The short poetic form of haiku was ideal for them, and they -both middle school and college students – actually produced some great haikus in the traditional format of 5-7-5 (five syllables, seven syllable, five syllables in a three-line stanza).

I called this particular stack, "My Kind of Haiku" because I constructed my own syllabic form, 7-9-3.

It is just two more syllables (19) than the traditional form.

After reading excellent overviews and examples of this Japanese poetic form, I found the book *Haiku in English* to be one of the most thoroughly written books on the subject. Compiled and edited by Kacian, Rowland, and Burns, this volume inspired me to continue experimenting with my 7-9-3 form. After reading varied haiku forms of over 300 English and American poets in *Haiku in English,* my confidence was raised in creating my own 7-9-3 constraint. In this volume, *Land Sea Earth Sky,* even though I have gone one syllable beyond the 19 in a few of the haikus, most adhere to the 7-9-3 syllabic construct.

Land Sea Earth Sky is a gift given to me by God. His still small voice woke me up with the title, gave me confidence to veer off the beaten haiku path and gave me the freedom to write in my own cadence. While looking through piles of finished poetry, He also told me not to use any of them. He gave me Luke 5:38, "But new wine must be put into new bottles; and both are preserved." He told me to use the other poems another way, at another time in another venue, but not for this project. Therefore, I wrote all of these new haikus under the inspiration of the Lord.

This book is divided into five sections: Land, Sea, Earth, Sky and a conglomerate section of Land, Sea, Earth, and Sky. I have provided a few photos that I took during some of my travels which I felt were relevant to each division. There is a scripture after each haiku to inspire others to delve further into God's Word. Unless otherwise indicated, all scripture is from the King James Version. A brief explanation and purpose of each division is as follows:

Land Sea Earth Sky

Part One: Land

Often the words "land" and "earth" are synonymous in the Bible, but frequently the word "land" indicates a specific geographical place for a specific people. It may also indicate the spiritual and physical condition of the people and their country, nation, city, or town. One instance is Abraham moving from the Land of the Chaldees (idol worshippers) to a land God promised him (worshippers of the True and Living God). Another instance is the effects that the people's spiritual condition have on the health of the land. If they were disobedient to God's Word, they might suffer famine or drought (Jeremiah 50:38). If they were obedient to his statutes, they would experience abundant rain and fruitful harvest (Isaiah 32:15). There are many references in the Bible to specific lands and ethnic groups such as the "land of Egypt", the "land of Canaan", the "land of the Philistines", and the "land of Israel", depicting national custom and spiritual

xv

relationship to God or the lesser gods. Other metaphorical expressions are "land of giants", the "land of corn", "land of milk and honey", "land of my kindred" and "land of the living", to name a few. These expressions often indicate the desirability of that land and its people and whether they are viewed as good or evil.

Part Two: Sea

The Sea is synonymous with "waters" which may include rivers, lakes, springs and brooks that either pour into the sea or are off-springs of the sea. The sea can be a great punisher as when the Pharaoh's army was drowned in the Red Sea (Exodus 14:28) or a great nurturer expressed in Psalm 104:25 as the life sustainer of "things innumerable, both small and great beasts". This large body of water can evoke metaphors and similes that represent abundance of population as "the sand of the sea" which God promised Abraham (Genesis

32:1-12), abundance of provision given to Joseph (Genesis 41:49), abundance of wealth given to the tribes of Israel (Deuteronomy 33:18-20) and abundance of knowledge as bestowed upon Solomon (I Kings 4:29). The sea can also represent beings and people of contention and evil (Revelation 13:1; 20:8) and an agent for the pardoning of sin, cleansing and forgiveness (Micah 7:19).

Part Three: Earth

"Earth" as opposed to "land" in this volume is used to depict the more universal meaning of Earth and is more concerned with its creation, its immensity and relationship to the even larger universe as well as with the individual as part of the universal scheme. It deals with human qualities common to all men in relationship to the natural and spiritual worlds. It over-rides the specificity of a group of people or nation.

Part Four: Sky

"Sky" and "Heaven" are often used interchangeably. The earthly sky and the heavenly hosts both interact with man. The earthly sky is used by God to warn, to bless or curse with the abundance or lack of the natural elements of rain, sleet, hail, and snow as well as clouds and wind. The sky that is visible to man is the abode of flying creatures of the natural and man-made world (birds, flying insects and man-made aircraft). It is sometimes the thoroughfare of supernatural creatures such as an appointed angel sent to earth to deliver a message to the mother of Christ, the angel that wrestled with Jacob, the angelic hosts who announced the birth of Christ, the cherubim of Ezekiel's vision and the dove that descended from heaven to rest on Christ. All of these supernatural beings and manifestations have "come down from heaven" using the portal of our earthly sky when God ordained it.

The words "heaven" or "heavens" are mentioned over 400 times in the Old Testament and over 200 times in the New Testament, occurring most frequently in the Books of Psalm, Matthew and Revelation. This is God's realm that also includes the mysteries of the planets, stars and constellations outside our solar system.

Part Five: Land, Sea, Earth, and Sky

This division serves as a summary of sorts. The elements of land, sea, earth and sky are intermingled in the haikus rather than being expressed separately as in the previous divisions. The purpose of this conglomeration is to show how interconnected we are within the microcosm of land, sea, earth and sky and how the vastness of God in his unsearchable wisdom is mindful of the macrocosm of the universes and constellations. This also shows His love and concern for the most wretched man (the possessed Gadarene), the most ostracized woman (Rahab the harlot), and the smallest beast (the ant). Conversely, He considers the most brilliant minds (Gamaliel), the strongest tree (trees of Lebanon), the fiercest animal (the lion), the brightest galaxies (Orion, Pleiades) — from the least to the greatest.

As Psalm 8:4-5 declares, "What is man, that thou art mindful of him? . . . For thou hast made him a little lower than the angels and crowned him with glory and honor". This is a messianic message; however, as receivers of Christ, we are covered by Romans 8:17, "And if children, then heirs; heirs of God, and joint-heirs with Christ; if so be that we suffer with him, that we may be also glorified together." Psalm 139:16 tells us we were in His book before we were conceived. His book is where He is–in Heaven. We came through this portal to abide just a little while within His *Land, Sea, Earth and Sky for His Purpose.*

PART ONE: LAND

Psalm 100:1-2

Make a joyful noise unto the Lord, all ye lands.

Serve the Lord with gladness: come before his

presence with singing.

Showpiece

Eden, a fruitful land once

To man, God's showpiece and perfection

Adam-Eve.

Genesis 3:9-11

Words

Land of Words bring death or life

To speak as silver apples in a

Golden bowl

Or slip a serpent in Life's

Tree where words seem shining

apple-ripe —

Death is sly.

Genesis 3:3-4; Proverbs 18:21

False Trees

Only ONE tree of life lives

The false ones sink to their roots,

    wailing loud

    "You *are* Lord!"

Romans 14:11

First

First, He will separate them

Wheat from tares, light from dark, good from evil

    Rock from Sand

Matthew 13:24-30,38

Unwashed Fruit

Obey your Lord, trees of Figs

If not, sinless lips can never taste

unwashed fruit.

Matthew 21:19-20

Like Grass

Grass is grass, man is like grass

Thriving in the moisture of morning

Gone by noon.

Psalm 37:1-2

Land of Bloods

We come from the land, our bloods
In the soil, our faces turned upward we
Must go home.

Genesis 3:19

Land of the King

Like Esther, I boldly stepped

In the land of the King, his scepter

Healed my heart.

Esther 5:1-3

Worthless Work

To build houses and watch walls

Without the hands and eyes of God is

Worthless work.

Continents sick with no God

Cities, countries, appear to bear

     fruit while

Souls decay

Psalm 127:1

Recognize

Mountains curtsy, ewes bow low

They join the orchards as they beat their

Tambourines

Lands! Recognize your God. Be

Diligent, be grateful He lets you

In His House

I Kings 18:37-39

DNA

He has written special plans

For his special needs children saved

Best for last

Our DNA is His great

Work unique to each cell's molecule

Land of flesh

Psalm 139:13-17

Let Us Pray

In this Land our minds are weak

We are dumb as mules that have

no speech

Wingless doves

Give back wings to fly the Land

Heal our vocal cords and bless our mouths

Let us pray.

2 Chronicles 7:14

Vesper-Time

Daylight and Vesper-time the

Sunflower opens to sunbeams and

Primrose to stars

I'm a Vesper-time creature

I grow at night roots in ground while I

Weep, Joy waits.

Psalm 30:5

Geniuses Think

Geniuses think thoughts they think

Are branches from their own trees forget

God makes trees

Isaiah 55:9

No Visible Sun

There is no visible Sun

On roots of trees yet in the dark they

Sprout with strength

2 Corinthians 4:18

New

Clean hearts right spirit rise up

As You, Lord, grow our grass, sow new

Seeds in us

Psalm 51:10

PART TWO: SEA

Genesis 1:10

. . . and the gathering together of the waters

called he Seas: and God saw that

it was good.

Sea-Child

Seas mind God. They do what He

Says: "Pile in a heap and let them

cross" or

"Drown them all."

Exodus 14:28-29

Sea-Womb

For God, the sea is a frame

That holds the earth in place like a womb

Holds its babe

Job 38:8-11

Pigs Jumped

You would not allow me, Lord,

To run through tombs, naked and howling

Like a dog

You gave me sanity's cloak

I wore it on my mind and pigs jumped

In the sea

Mark 5:13

Peculiar

Seas are peculiar waters

They sparkle and lay calm in the sun

Then they roar.

Psalm 89:9

Land Sea Earth Sky

Erased

Waters we know erase from

Eyes as we, the Bride of Christ, don our

Wedding Clothes

Revelation 4:6-7

Land Sea Earth Sky

Old Mysteries

Seas conceal old mysteries

We called some dinosaurs what God named

Leviathan

Psalm 104:26

Behemoth Bones

Our museums hold their bones

In captivity, but they bathed in

God's waters

Behemoth and the Dragon

Drank up His mighty floods with joy,

Then — Disappeared.

Job 40:15, 23

Feet Walking

Galilee Sea felt Feet walk

softly on its back heard men cry *storm*

Shut its mouth

Its waves could not buck against

His Heel-it did not want to. God told

It to rest.

Matthew 14:22-27; Mark 4:39-41

The Birthing Sea

It is a majestic thing

The birthing sea, huge whales, small

    fish from

Waters' loins

Majestic thing, the birthing

Sea where millions spew her birth canal —

The mouth of God

    Psalm 104:25-27

Counterfeits

Daniel saw visions of four

Beasts coming out of the Sea to hurt

The whole earth

Counterfeits trying to be

Like God, rule like God, sit as God, be

Judged by God.

Daniel 7:3-7

Casting His Net

Jesus found them casting their

Nets for fish Peter and Andrew, His

Eyes on them

His soul on them, searching by

The Sea of Galilee, caught their hearts

Before Times

Matthew 4:18-19

PART THREE: EARTH

Genesis 1:12

And the earth brought forth grass, and herb yielding seed after his kind, and the Tree yielding fruit, whose seed was in itself, after his kind: and God saw that it was good.

After Our Kind

We produce after our kind

Wrath to wrath, grace to grace, face to face

    Our *own* kind

I am your seed, Lord, let me

Produce after Your kind, not yeasted bread

    But pure loaf

John 6:35; 1 Corinthians 5:8

Seeing Blind

When God chooses to show us

Ourselves, we place dark shades on eyes that

   see blind things

   The tongue thinks it's the eye

   The ear thinks it's the nose we hear wrong

   And Speak dumb.

Matthew 13:15

Replacement

Lily of the valley smells like Love

In fields of Redemption worlds of grace

Thorns replaced

Song of Solomon 2:1-2

God's Grip

Bears and lions like ragdolls, were
In David's grip, succumbed to greater
Than David.

I Samuel 17:37

Your Guts

Drink the cup with biting wine

And eat with a King that hates your guts

    Vomit up.

           Proverb 23:6-8

The Beautiful Ball

Earth was empty, without form

A burnt out ball, God made beautiful

Just for us

Genesis 1:2

Baby-steps Out-side

Babies roll, squirm, crawl, then walk

I took baby-steps outside this World

No more child

I Corinthians 13:11

Deep

Before *we* knew, *Isaiah*

Knew Earth was a circle hung by God

Heaven-deep

Isaiah 40:22

Master of Peace

God's Show-Piece became His shame

Fig leaves disgraced, God sent His

Son, His

Master-Peace

John 3:16

Tough Love

In the cool shaded Garden

Of God's delight, they thought they

could hide

From tough love.

Genesis 3:24

Ordinary I

Ordinary dust like us

Were made to open seas, float axes,

Bring down fire.

turn the sky black and cause hail

stones to strike the palaces of Kings

In the Earth

I Kings 18:36, 38

Ordinary II

Cleanse the leper and fill empty

Pots with oil for widows and snatch a

Child from death.

I Kings 17:23; 2 Kings 5:10

Ordinary III

Gave power to His dust to

Stop the Sun and block the clouds from

Raining rain

I Kings 18:41-44

Lamb, Coin, Son

Lamb, coin, son — all lost but found

Shepherd searched, woman swept,

father wept

God's Word kept.

Luke 15: 6, 9, 24

Clean

In a ditch with wolves that looked

    like sheep, God's hook found my neck

    and brought

        me out clean.

Divine rewards from You, Lord:

    Kind escapes, a breath from death, a child's

    Loving arms

       I Corinthians 10:13

Hungry

With hungry forks and knives, we

Eat Your Spirit, with thirsting lips we

Drink it up

Matthew 5:6

Ones Like Me

Thank you God for lending me
A corner of earth, a precious grain
This, myself

Your earth-ward compassion loved
The ones -once the other side of You-
Ones like me.

Psalm 139:13-15

Pure Child's Play

Children's tongues in pure child's play

Tell grownups what God's thinking

and they

Dream God's thoughts

Psalm 8:2

Old Bones

Sarah and Abraham shared

Their bed in faith, from old bones to young

Isaac sprung

Genesis 17:17, 21:2

Land Sea Earth Sky

Where is Your Sword, Lord?

They came from under the altar

Blood-washed they died a beheaded death

Praised His Name

How long they cried, *how long Lord*

We have on our robes of righteousness

Where is your Sword?

Revelation 6:10-11

Assurance

In love He assures them as

They stand waiting, knowing His

sword will

Soon be pulled.

Revelation: 7:13-17; Romans 1:18

Wondrous Things

Four wondrous things on the Earth

Pleases God, perplexes man, eagle's

flight through clouds

The way pure women woo men

The way a serpent moves on rocks and

Ships sail seas

Proverbs 30:18-19

Unbearable things

Four things the earth cannot stand

An unsatisfied woman who weds

A meek man

A fool full of food and wine

Babbling silly words and drunk with

Selfishness

A coveting servant who

Rises to reign and a maid that's heir

To her Queen.

Proverbs 30:21-23

Tiny Things

Four Tiny things In the Earth

God made them small but wise, weak

      but strong

Rulers none.

Little ant people that build

Twice their size and spiders that lodge in

Royal rooms.

The microscopic Conies

Make mansions in rocks and Locust have

No captain.

Proverbs 30:24-28

Amazing Things

Earth displays four amazing

Things even God sits back to watch their

Comeliness

Lion' s prance and flowing mane

The greyhound's speed, the he-goat's

 stance, and

Fearless kings.

Proverbs 30:29-31

Justice

When His spirit became His

Son in the earth His Mercy became

His Justice

Romans 5:8

Molded

I am a miracle made

With Christ-molded parts, breathed

up my soul

A blessed wind

Genesis 2:7; Job 33:4

Verbs and Nouns

Born to perform mighty things

We are Verbs living in a Noun world

Work His Works!

Philippians 4:13

Balance

God's great business vengeance is

Ups and downs, backs and forths

Hearts found out

Romans 12:19

Until

Day and Night is forever

Seasons will not move until God gives

His Final Call

Genesis 8:22; 2 Peter 3:10

PART FOUR: SKY

Psalm 8:3-4

When I consider thy heavens, the work of

thy fingers, the moon and the stars, which

thou hast ordained;

What is man, that thou art mindful of him?

and the son of man, that thou visitest him?

Daystar

Shepherd of the Sheep, Daystar

Came down, sent Himself, fixed

Himself clothed

Virgin-wrapped

Philippians 2:6-8

Lame Lambs

I cannot, I will not be

An afterthought or take lame lambs, I AM

Heaven's Lord

King of skies, Master Maker

I own the clouds, possess the winds, I

Wake Pleiades

Deuteronomy 15:21; Psalm 103:2

Pure Rain

Fresh rain has fallen where I

Fell, crushed, seared where serpents

stung my soul

Pure rain healed.

2 Samuel 23:4; Hosea 6:3

They Were Four

Ezekiel, John saw the four

Beast come down from Heaven and

they were

Divine beasts.

Creatures of the Highest God

Adoring Him Day and Night, kneeling

At His Throne.

Revelation 5:8

Land Sea Earth Sky

Two Days

One thousand years is a day

In the Kingdom of the King and His Prince

Two days gone.

II Peter 3:8

Kingdom Come

When Jesus Christ rips the sky

CNN and Internet will see

Kingdom's come.

Eyes open clear-wide stars fall

From the womb of the sky while lands wail,

Princes hide

Revelation 5:13

Angels Sang

Sages saw the Star afar

But angels sang to shepherds and sheep

From Heaven

Luke 2:13-15; Matthew 2:9-10

Hang-Glide

Rode that chariot, reins tight

Elijah showed we, too, might hang-glide

The Firmament

2Kings 2:11

Land Sea Earth Sky

To Cleanse

To heaven's face Rainbow smiled

Promised Earth no more floods to

    cleanse now

Fire waits.

Genesis 9:13-15

Still

Between wars and high-jacked planes

Missing children and whistling

drones, Grace

Still trumps sin.

Romans 5:20

No Never

Timelessness, where God resides,

Has no Before, no After, no Next

No Never

Revelation 10:6

Ezekiel's Sight I

From the corner of my eye

I saw them move, six wings they had and

Four faces

Down from heaven's heights, they came

To me, mere flesh on bone they

showed their

Strength in flight.

Ezekiel 10:19

Ezekiel's Sight II

And I, prophet Ezekiel,

Asked God, questioned God, feared

    His answer

Feared His call.

Saw the creatures in their might

Feared the one who made these

    ultra things

With six wings.

Ezekiel 10:18

Land Sea Earth Sky

Ezekiel's Sight III

Who am I from the earth's soil
What privilege that I should peek this
Sacred sight!

Six wings, and wheels burning, four
Faces and voices like a thousand
Waterfalls.

Ezekiel 1:3, 24

Ezekiel's Sight IV

On each creature, four faces

An angel's, an eagle's, a lion's

And man's face.

Their God is a mighty God

Who *is my* God, a *powerful* God

Lord. I bow.

Ezekiel 10:12-14

War Clothes

When He rose up to Heaven, grave
clothes gone, we graduated from the
House of Hell.

Put your War Clothes on straight from
the sky, let your Fighting Garments make
Demons cry

Ephesians 6:12-13

What Do We Play?

Are we notes in flights of brass

Key boards of discord, hurting sounds in

Atmosphere?

Or are we God's melodies

Drums of joy, harps of love, trumpets of

His Glory?

I Corinthians 1:1; Psalm 150

Gifts

Man's inventions are God's thoughts

Sent on airwaves in dreams as gifts to

Those who seek.

James 1:17

By Order of the Lord

Sun and Moon by order of

The Lord, you must watch over me, your

     Assignment's clear

Moon, your light protect me in

Thickest night and Sun, you rise to blind

My enemies

Psalm 121:6-7

Skies of Day

In Heaven's light years exist

No yesterday-tomorrow's night— just

Skies of Day

Revelation 21:25; Revelation 22:5

God Loves

God loves the whore because He

Waits for her wounded heart to answer

When He knocks

She let down the scarlet rope

And brought up heaven to her

house where

Christ came through

Joshua 6:22-25; Hebrews 11:31

Gifts that Ride

Man's inventions God's thoughts true

Gifts that ride upon airwaves in dreams

Through babes' tongues

Daniel 1:17; Matthew 21:15-16; Matthew 11:25

Manna

Jesus from skies descended

Manna, bread of Heaven served himself

Eat His Life.

John 6:48-50

Righteous Song

Horns blow for You, Lord, trumpets
Triumphant, celestial harps strum Your
Righteous Song

Psalm 98:5-6; Psalm 150:3

PART FIVE: LAND, SEA, EARTH, SKY

John 1:1-3

In the beginning was the Word, and the Word

was with God, and the Word was God.

The same was in the beginning with God.

All things were made by him; and without him

was not anything made that was made.

From Nowhere

Land, Sea, Earth, Sky made in days

ordained to spaces out from nowhere

Ancient New

Job 26:7; Revelation 21:1-3

Looking

My flesh is my land made by You
And like Your Land Sea Earth and Sky, I
Groan and wait.

On tip-toes we look for You
From grand Orion to smallest beasts
We long for You.

Romans 8:23-24

Ask?

Land, Sea Earth Sky, can we ask

Why? As created realms from God's Sound

No. Not yet.

I Corinthians 13:12

Death Coat

Fools say God is dead, but when

He shakes the Milky Way, lies will wear

The coat of Death

And there will be no question

Who is Lord of Land, Sea, Earth, Sky, Us

   Universe

Psalm 14:1-3

Mine

They are all mine God resounds

    Opulent fields, pregnant clouds, pearls in

    Swamp mud. Mine

Gardens and lakes worship Me

Orchards and Mountains with rivers

    and springs

    Dance My days

    Romans 14:11

They Know

Lambs and bulls, oxen and bees
Roses, lilies and sweet grapevines, God
Says *All Mine*

They submit, desert, Salt Sea
Man-made brick and tempered steel
      bend low
See. They know.

Isaiah 45:23

Always

Always Is, always Was, not

Just Light of *our* Land, *our* Sea, *our*

Earth, *our* Sky

Always shall be Light and Life

Of galaxies, constellations, stars,

Suns unknown

Philippians 2:10; Revelation 21:1;

Isaiah 44:24

No Fear

In the tumults of Land, Sea

Earth and Sky, my ear is near His heart

Beat. No fear.

Joshua 1:9

Think My

Think I ask the springs for drink

Seek advice from brains I made think *My*

Dead won't live?

Think My sword won't swipe and cleanse

Think I forget sweet smells of prayers

From *My* Saints?

Revelation 5:8

Perfection

Perfect was – Land sea earth sky

First Adam obeyed first Eve and made the

Whole World die

Genesis 1:26-28; Genesis 2:19-20; I

Corinthians 15:21-22, 26

Falling Birds

Before we drown or hit ground

Before our wings break, Your Net

    swoops up

Falling birds

Luke 12:5-7

If We don't Praise Him

If we don't praise Him seas will

Leap, clouds will laugh and rocks will

shout with

Cherubim

Psalm 98:7-8

Printed in the USA
CPSIA information can be obtained
at www.ICGtesting.com
LVHW022000121023
760667LV00003B/7

9 781498 435222